Francis M.] [from old catalog] [English

Prohibition

A Fallacy, A Fanaticism, And An Absurdity

Francis M.] [from old catalog] [English

Prohibition
A Fallacy, A Fanaticism, And An Absurdity

ISBN/EAN: 9783742898272

Manufactured in Europe, USA, Canada, Australia, Japa

Cover: Foto ©ninafisch / pixelio.de

Manufactured and distributed by brebook publishing software (www.brebook.com)

Francis M.] [from old catalog] [English

Prohibition

PROHIBITION

A FALLACY, A FANATICISM,

AND AN

ABSURDITY.

CONTRARY TO THE CONSTITUTION OF THE UNITED STATES.

THE LAWS OF CREATION, CIVILIZATION, COMMON SENSE AND RATIONAL PROGRESS,

---

BECAUSE

Contrary to the Teachings of the

BIBLE.

---o---

JERSEYVILLE, ILL:
COMMERCIAL BOOK AND JOB PRINTING OFFICE.
1890.

Entered according to Act of Congress, in the year 1891, by
FRANCIS M. ENGLISH,
In the office of the Librarian of Congress, at Washington, D. C.

PREFACE.

———o———

In offering this small volume for the eye of all that read for the purpose of being benefitted, and satisfied in the acquisition of information of value, our subject and its analysis will interest, satisfy and benefit every one capable of deducing from the premises conclusions demonstrated by sound reasoning from undisputed facts. This book supplies a thorough analysis or exegesis of the teachings of the Book of Inspiration, on the subject of temperance in all its diversified bearings. Whether or not the Bible favors, by suggestion or command, that human statutes should or should not be provided to prevent the possibility of the excessive use of intoxicants by statutory inhibition, so that under any circumstances it would not be possible for any man, woman or minor ever to become intoxicated. We believe that the Bible is as silent on the question of prohibition statutory legislation to *prevent* the possibility of inebriation as it is to prevent adultery, fornication, uncleanness, lasciviousness, idolatry, witchcraft, hatred, variance, emulations, wrath, strife, seditions, heresies, envyings, murders, revelings and such like. In this catalogue of offences against

God's moral government—is *drunkenness*. St. Paul says, "they that *do such things shall not* inherit the kingdom of God." Galatians, 5 ch, 19-21 v. Philanthropic and profoundly pious christian prohibionists see nothing in this chain of flagrant practices to claim their consideration and denunciation but drunkenness—not a whit worse immorality than any others denounced. This small volume will furnish the reader with ample compensation for its expense, and the time necessary to examine its claim upon the confidence of all that are capable of deducing from reliable premises and undisputed facts, conclusions commanding their ready and unhesitating approval.

   To all concerned,
    Respectfully,
     FRANCIS M. ENGLISH.
JERSEYVILLE, ILL.,
 January 1, 1891.

PROHIBITION A FALLACY.

The principle, fanaticism, seeks to have formulated into law; by State and National legislation—for the government of the voluntary conduct of men different from the universally accepted moral laws of civilization, should be commended by authority that all concerned could approve, advocate and defend.

The code of ethics demanded by prohibitionists, does not and never did exist, by the sanction of the Bible, and constitutional law, because it would subvert and destroy the rule by which mankind were to govern themselves in the gift, and as the condition of their creation; and would nullify the assumption that they were capable of self-government and not morally responsible for their voluntary actions, to any law human or divine.

A law that a rational man or woman cannot violate, is no law at all. It would be nothing but brute force, a chain upon the ankles and a yoke around the neck.

The man or woman in the exercise of their divinely endowed freedom of will, that could not be tempted to do as their choice might prompt whether right or wrong, and be responsible for the consequences of praise or blame, God, never created.

A law of legal prohibition (prevention) of the use of any and every substance, natural or manufactured, as a beverage or palatal gratification, that might from excessive use intoxicate, is of modern origin, fanatical in conception, impracticable in operation, because absurd in its demand. Legislation that would attempt to abate or remove the cause of any immoral act, (intemperance is an immoral act) would be without a statute to enforce it, an example to illustrate its application, and destitute of any merit to command respect.

Nothing of the kind appears in the legislation of Jehovah, from Adam in the Garden to Moses on the Summit, where the great leader of Isreal received the *Statutes of the world* from the fiery hands of the great God Himself. Statutes that have never been repealed nor amended, and never will be, while there is a fish to swim in the sea, a bird to sail through the air, a star to twinkle in the heavens or while the earth shall yield a plant, the ocean roll a wave, or the sun shall give his light by day and the moon continues to shine at low twelve. These statutes to regulate the moral conduct of men were in force from the beginning, up to the funeral obsequies of the last prophet that ever uttered a rule for their enforcement for the government of men.

Next was John the Baptist, whose relation to all the Old Testament prophets was that of Jupiter to the planetary kingdom, the greatest of all the subordinate hosts that shine.

Nothing in John's dispensation appears to support the modern heresy of legal prohibition,—the statutory prevention of the existence and rational use of intoxicants.

From the burning bush in Midian, where Moses beheld the green shrub in flames, but unconsumed, to the communion of the one hundred and twenty in the upper chamber in Jerusalem; not a statute can be found to support the absurdity that gospel temperance prohibitionists demand.

Nor from the benediction of the last supper, where the redeeming Christ touched the wine cup of sacramental remembrance to the lips of the immortal twelve, to the closing vision of John upon the lonely Isle of Patmos, no such interdiction is intimated, in the evangelical and apostolic teachings.

Yet inspiration thunders and blazes with injunction and restraint, not to use intoxicants intemperately—to excess; with penal consequence as frightful as flames, and without repentance as dreadful as eternal retribution.

But, the fanaticism of prohibitionists demand that state and national enactment, must abate—prohibit—prevent, the occasion (not the cause) of drunkeness, that intemperance may universally and forever cease. To illustrate the absurdity of prohibition, the principle of it is this: That whereas for business, profit and pleasure, the bosom of the rivers, lakes, seas and oceans, have been burdened with crafts of steam and sail and mechanical appliances for centuries, the incidental consequences of which, millions of lives have been imperilled and sacrificed, and billions of treasure forever lost to its owners, and to the commerce of the world; therefore they should be prohibited—prevented.

The great apostle Paul, the hero of Athens, and confounder of the Areopagite, was a passenger and a prisoner on one of these commercial agencies, when the entire cargo was lost, and the proud monarch of the seas surrendered to the vengeance of the tempest, and two hundred and seventy-six human lives were jeopardised for many days on account of the unabated violence of the storm, insomuch that all hope of escaping a watery tomb vanished. Acts, 27 Chap. If you please, think of the lives and treasure that have perished in consequence of the use of the Ohio and Mississippi rivers alone, as the pathways of pleasure, business and profit during the last hundred years in the use of the thousands of devices in the interest of rational want and necessity, from the canoe, skiff, ferry and freight-boats, keel and barges up to the grand steam-propelling palaces whose thundering waves have shaken the slumbering shores of the Mississippi, and floated driftwood, corks and corn-stalks on the Ohio for nearly a century.

The principles of legal prohibition teach, that such disasters should be prohibited: Not by legislation that all such crafts shall perform their functions by agencies capable of securing to rational men and women, all the benefits of pleasure and profit involved in their use in the lawful pursuits of life; with such penalties as will oblige fidelity to such legislation; but the legislation, the principle of prohibitionists—is to abate these natural, and artificial provisions—mankind's rational wants demand. Their logic is this: That no proud craft of steam or sail may ever again blow up, burn up, capsize or sink; on account of which lives and treasures may be lost or destroyed; from source to confluence, or from the Monongahela and the Alleghany, with every stream that contributes to press its shores and deepen its channel, from Pittsburg to Cairo—the Ohio must be dried up, or in some way destroyed; then steam, and other boat disasters will surcease forever.

Such are legitimate deductions from the reasoning of politico–religio–fanatical–gospel temperance prohibitionists. This brood of par-excellent philanthropic moralists have become bold; assuming perfection in morals and a degree in christian attainment above all others not of their sentiment and purpose. They denounce all connected with the "infernal liquor traffic" as they call it, as "murderers!" Inhumanity the principle that governs them.

Inexcusable depravity their habits, and hell their destination. Because they fail to shout great is the Diana they worship, gospel temperance prohibition, achievable only by statutory—human legislation. If inebriation may be prevented, (not prohibited, for drunkeness is already prohibited—forbidden with penalty, so far as God has ever legislated on the subject) may not the same authority obliterate the entire catalogue of immoral offences? If not, why?

The Bible is admitted an all sufficient rule of faith and practice for the government of all men, regardless of nationality, or any other circumstantial condition, and whatever is not taught therein can be inferred therefrom, and proven thereby, is not to be received, but rejected as heretical and without the demands of God Himself, whose statutes are perfect for the government of mankind—to the end of the world. They are perspicuous on the question of temperance, wherein not a suggestion is made—from Genesis to Revelations, by patriarchs, prophets, John the Baptist, the Redeeming Christ, His Evangelists and Apostles, that local option, total abstinence or statutory prohibition, is any part of his revealed will. They *demand* TEMPERANCE in every dispensation from all men, with ample ·penalties to restrain from offending and to provoke ready and cheerful obedience and nothing more.

As the pulpit with its cognate alliances, the co-operation of all civil enactments from Theodosius and Justinian to the present time, encouraged by such moral suasion, and has failed to accomplish ends demanded by prohibitionists, is it safe or wise to set aside such agencies and depend upon the uncertain, the unreliable will of a legislation, controlled by the corrupt sentiments of partisan politics to effect—by unconstitutional enactments—not required, not commanded by divine authority, a result the combined forces mentioned have proved inadequate to achieve.

In all this inflammatory crusade against the "infernal liquor traffic" as the assumed piety or philanthropy of prohibitionists call it, the epitaph of defeat remains upon its unwrinkled brow; yet it is ignorantly or insanely presumed that state and national legislation would be the panacea.

From the days of Dio Lewis, the originator and organizer of the church women's praying and singing crusade against the saloons by which Lewis reaped a financial harvest in the sale of his so called temperance books, it has been manifest—with some exceptions that the distinguished itinirant hireling temperance harranguers have been influenced more by the motive of financial compensation for services rendered, or for political notoriety in hope of official distinction through this depraved instrumentality, than to "save the drunkard from the drunkard's grave."

Remember St. John and Gen. Fisk, candidates for presidential honors, with $50,000 a year, if accidentally successful dazzling to their gaze. And where is the father and his "talented boys," the Murphy? with their budget of laughable anecdotes and sycophantical motto, "We have malice towards none and charity for all." They are yet in the field. Who cares or is concerned for either their charity or malice. Their equals in all respects, not to say their superiors as good citizens and christians are engaged in the liquor traffic. And who cares or is concerned for either their charity or malice in their mercenary pilgrimage throughout the states, with the pulpit pew, Sabbath school children and temperance organizations, the W. C. T. U. shouting their approach and compensating their service with a bank account far beyond that in reach of their time and talents given to any other calling.

When benevolent and beneficent labors come from the promptings that it pays better than any thing else in which I can engage my time and talents, superior intelligence and moral honesty should except to the pretentious assumptions of such imposters and impositions, and protest the demands upon popular credence, and for undeserved financial remuneration.

From the beginning of public efforts, more than half a century ago, to relieve society of disturbing inebriation—to the extent then common—public and domestic, by odds less than now, and to restore to sobriety all that might have been, or might be over come by excessive indulgence in intoxicants, nothing was more appropriate and commendible, than public addresses, and newspaper literature—asserting the demands of inspiration that all men should "live soberly" "be sober" and to "be not drunk with wine wherein is excess". * The work of temperance reformation was originally from the pulpit of the churches, especially the Methodist Church, whose discipline disallowed membership to any who indulged dram-drinking and drunkeness, and would not repent."

* It is the excess and not the use of the wine that is forbidden.

At first temperance lectures were cognates of ministerial labors. The preachers were required by conference resolves to preach expressly on temperance. This habit became diffusive and the pulpits of the churches generally entertained their congregations periodically with temperance sermons. The monstrosity of legal prohibition was slow of incubation, such fanaticism was sluggish in its manifestation. It was a hybrid of questionable qualities in its first conception. It demanded as a condition for its birth and baptism, a low grade of political depravity, and mercenary stimulation into a tangible entity.

It is a bald-headed and dough-faced misnomer for a christian morality, that it is necessary for men (some men) to be christians they must be placed by civil legislation beyond the possibility of being tempted to become inebriates. It was stated by a doctor of divinity on the floor of annual conference as his reason why he favored a resolution asking the state legislature to enact a prohibitory law and that the conference should forbid anything but *sweet* wine for sacramental purposes, that he had a member in his station who was started on a spree from the stimulation of the sacramental cup at every communion.

But church patronage, with the special zeal of the church-women becoming politicians soon popularized the temperance specialty of public lecturing on temperance, insomuch it offered a field for usefulness for, here and there, a gifted orator, with a stipulated salary to give harrangues on temperance rather than to preach the gospel and call the mourners as aforetime.

But not the pulpit alone has supplied the temperance lecture field with shining intellects of the highest intelligence to enforce the Bible demands of temperance, but many, if not every state in the Union, has had its representation from the field and forge, from the bench of the jurist, and from the bar of the barrister. And the offices of the healing art have not been delinquent in contributions to temperance lecture fields; all pleading the cause of temperance to prevent their fellow men from being overcome by "tarrying too long" at, and drinking too deeply from the cup of intoxication. Upon this altar Kentucky—besides many others, within a half century, has offered up its Thomas F. Marshall, the Jupiter in the constellation of Kentucky's oratorical splendors.

His forensic blade was as keen as was ever unsheathed before the ermine of any judicial bench or lacerated the guilty conscience of a perjured incumbent upon the witness stand, or bribed juryman sworn to a seat in the legal panel.

This star of magnitude once traversed his native state as a temperance lecturer. The brilliance of his orations, the grandeur of his conceptions, the perspicuity of his incisive logic, the invulnerability of his arguments, the cyclonic sweep of his impassioned eloquence winged to sublimest heights, by his inflammatory zeal, in the grand work of reclaiming the "addicted" and to prevent the sober from the attractions of the intoxicating cup are still remembered by the thousands, while long ago he began his slumbers in the seclusion and solitude of uninterrupted death.

But our object in this treatise is not to disgust patience, and stupify the understanding, burden the memory and bewilder the imagination, by elaboration in the array of authorities and the detail of facts that temperance in all thing is philosophically correct, and demanded throughout the Book of Inspiration as indispensibly necessary to the welfare of every member of the human race.

But the main—central object, the controlling thought—is to answer the question, does the Bible teach the doctrine of political prohibition (statutory prevention) of the existence of any and every substance—the gift of nature—or the result of manufacture, so that inebriation will forever be impossible.

We deny that the Bible teaches such a doctfine, and assert that it is contrary to the teachings of the Bible.

Not a protest against the existence and use of intoxicants can be found in any chapter or verse of inspiration as the means of preventing the *abuse* of the *rational* use of intoxicants. Hence the fanaticism of prohibitionists in their attempt to ignore, set aside and abandon the Bible, as a code of morals, wholly inadequate in its injunctions and restraints, with awards to obedience bright as a well grounded hope of immortality can inspire; and with penalties for disobedience as dreadful as the vengeance of eternal retribution; and instead, human legislation must be evoked, not for the execution of God's moral laws, but to have instituted a new rule for men's moral government not mentioned in any part of the entire volume of inspiration.

Such morally insane conceptions would suggest that the Great God, and father of the human race, had been either reprehensibly careless, inexcusably indifferent or wholly incompetent to provide adequate laws for the government of His own intelligences, called men and women.

Get the exact size with every feature of a full grown pharisee, as delineated in the scriptures, and you have the photograph of modern prohibition gospel—temperance lecturers.

We will now proceed to present for the honest consideration of all disposed to pursue the subsequent pages of this small volume, every text in the Bible, giving, as we believe, its exact meaning, as it was intended to be understood, that bears directly or remotely upon the use of intoxicants. The reader, therefore, will be compensated far beyond the cost of the book, as it constitutes an encyclopædia or concordance of the texts in the Bible, that refer to the subject, not one of which teaches the doctrine of prohibition, local option, or total abstinence, either expressly by precept or example or by implication. Yet, in a great many of which, intoxication is forbidden, prohibited, but not *prevented,* and, in many others, unqualifiedly with severest penalty condemned.

As there is no other publication of the kind known to the author, he has been so thorough in the examination of the scriptures on the subject, that it can be relied upon as a text book as to what the Bible teaches on the question of temperance. What then is said in the Bible—both the Old and New testament scriptures, bearing on the use of intoxicants, no matter by what title given, whether wine, the vinegar of wine, strong drink or the vinegar of strong drink; any chemical substance, the gift of nature or artificial compound or manufacture, that by excessive use might intoxicate to the extent of superinducing drunkeness?

First then, attention is directed to the inebriation by excessively using wine, of one of the best men that ever lived. See Genesis, 19 ch.. 30-38 v. Here you have the momentous history of Lot. His purity of character was his divinely recognized shield against the destructive fire that cremated or reduced to ashes every existing thing—including every human being—male and female, man, woman and child that breathed the breath of life in Sodom and Gomorroh, excepting only himself, wife and two daughters; and in their escape from the vengeance of consuming flames, Lot's faith and fidelity of character was superior to that of his wife's, who for a cause known only to herself, "looked back and became a pillar of salt."

Yet in a brief period afterwards this illustrious man, around whose brow had encircled the glory of divine approbation, was found in a cave not far distant from his homestead, the little City of Zoar, so brutally drunk that he was oblivious to the presence of his remaining family—consisting of only his two grown daughters, entirely unconscious of being a *particip criminis* to moral offences a thousand fold more disasterous to his own personal character and that of his daughters, than to have been drunk for a thousand times. But prohibitionists may claim that the disaster that befell Lot and his daughters was caused by wine. Not a word of it. The wine was only the *occasion* and not the *cause*, any more than the "forbidden fruit" was the cause of the down-fall of Eve or that Eve was the cause of the down-fall of Adam. Eve was the *occasion* of Adam's fall, the fruit and the devil were the occasions but not the cause of Eve's fall. The wine was the *occasion* and not the *cause* of Lot's disaster to himself and daughters—steam was never the cause of boiler explosions by which thousands of lives have been destroyed.

The conflagration that years ago destroyed Chicago, was not the *cause* of the destruction only the *occasion*.

There is as distinct a difference in the ethical import of the terms *cause* and *occasion* as agencies in prompting a voluntary act, good or bad, as there is in the difference between an icicle and a coal of fire. And there is as much sense in charging that the forbidden fruit and the devil were the cause of Eve's fall—and that Eve was the *cause* of Adam's fall, as to charge that wine was the cause of the catastrophe to Lot and his daughters.

It was not the old cow, the milk-shed, the milk-maid nor the upset lamp that caused the destruction of Chicago. *Failure* to *extinguish* the fire before it reached the destructive vengeance of a conflagration was the cause. Nor was it the old cow, nor the milk shed, nor the milk-maid, nor the lamp containing the source of the conflagration that *caused* the destruction of Chicago. They were but the *occasion*. Each separte element was a good thing. The inflammatory qualities of the milk-shed, the milk-maid's placing the lamp in such relation to the heels of the cow that her unexpected kick upset it, then the combustible of the shed took fire that continued until the city was in ruins. The improper handling of the lamp by the milk-maid was the *cause* of the disaster.

It would not do to demand that statutory legislation must prohibit—prevent, the existence of a milk-shed, coal oil lamp, a milch-cow and a milk-maid, because of the possibility of a disaster to property and life by a milk-maid's incorrectly handling a coal-oil lamp when she had to milk after night. Handle intoxicants correctly and no more harm will be done than would have been the result had the milk-maid used the lamp properly. But, two points we wish to make against the heresy and fanaticism of prohibitionists from the biblical and logical standpoint. God did not prevent Eve from being tempted nor her surrender to temptation, nor did He prevent Lot from becoming intoxicated. Secondly; that intoxicants existed in the days of Lot, as certainly as that the forbidden fruit and the devil existed in the days of Eve. Thirdly; nor did there exist in the days of Eve and Lot, a law, such as prohibitionist are now seeking to have enacted by state and the national legislation for the moral government of men.

NOAH.

Next we review the case of Noah. Genesis 9-20-24 v. In this detail we have the comprehensive portrait of the oldest "preacher of righteousness" that ever lived—before or since the flood. His ministry continued for one hundred and twenty years. And, to the end of his momentous life, not a shadow of blemish or reproof of moral deficiency or delinquency rests upon his character, excepting only the one instance of inexcusable intoxication mentioned in the text. So consecrated in faith and practice, to God's revealed will, that he enjoyed the divine favor in so full a degree that, at the end of his ministry, while the reverberating thunders were echoing in alarming import above his devoted head, and an imparalleled rain fall was indicated by lightnings that flashed upon his bewildered vision, shattering into fragments the sturdy oaks and stately poplars that had reigned as forest kings in the valleys and upon the mountains for a thousand years as evidence of divine partiality and approval, it was whispered into his ears from above the pathway of the raging storm and falling waters that submerged every thing growing and green and extinguished the breath and destroyed the life of every human being of men women and children, that his servant, Noah, his wife, his three sons and their wives should escape the general disaster, which would be effected by a life-preserver, called the Ark. This device by divine instruction he had prepared for the result now to be achieved. At the end of this miraculous overflow, Noah and his household are safely anchored upon the top of the mountain, Ararat, whose summit was far above the wildest waves of the destroying deluge.

Then, after such manifestations of the divine favor to himself and family, and while they were the only representatives of the race of mankind on the face of all the earth, and while the wails of the dying and the agonizing groans of man and beast in their struggle against such an overwhelming ruin, were still echoing in every breath of the wind, burdening his ears with the sorrows of the dead imperishably sepulchered in his memory! Among the first products of the soil—responsive to his own hand—in its cultivation and before time and circumstances had contributed to his necessities sufficiently to provide a comfortable homestead, his vineyard supplied him with the stimulating extract of the grape, ample to overcome his sobriety by excessive indulgence and he is to be seen in his tent in a state of exhausting demoralizing intoxication.

That no fanatical prohibitionist, or, any one else, may charge that the color in our rainbow that encircles the scene we delineate are too strongly tinctured with imaginary hues, we direct the eyes of all that may doubt the fidelity of our portrait, to examine the dyes and brush with which we have thrown the picture upon the canvas for observation. The text says, "And Noah began to be a husbandman and he planted a vineyard, and he drank of the wine, and was drunken, and he was uncovered within his tent.— And Noah awoke from his wine &c."

The prohibitionist is requested to read the entire details of this remarkable event in the history of a great and good man; and he may see that there was then, as now, other ways for men to sin besides using intoxicants to excess. And another impression may be made that the great God did not denounce Noah as a beast and brute for this reprehensible indiscretion and avoidable weakness. Nor did he then and there institute a prohibitory law for Noah's future government. There is nothing in prohibition but fanaticism and absurdity.

We presume from the days of Noah to the day of grace, A. D. 1890, the great God has remained the same in all the qualities and attributes of his eternal nature, so that what was offending to his moral law then, is still the subject of his disapproval.

Nothing in the qualities of man's nature has changed demanding a new rule for the moral government of men. Such being the undisputed facts in the case what respect can be challenged from anyone, saint or sinner, for the opinions of that remarkable product of pulpit notoriety at nearly the close of the 19th century, A. D. 1890, in the person and ministerial pretensions of the Rev. Sam Jones. From many of the pulpit utterances of this distinguished representative of the sacred desk, (pulpit) a sample of which is hereto attached, he has been awarded the sobriquet of an ecclesiastical blackguard, with a sad and radical departure from the standard of dignity, self respect and a civilized estimate of the feelings of the audiences he has had the opportunity and honor to publicly address, as an accredited preacher of the gospel of the redeeming Christ. Meekness, humanity. and forbearing patience in reproving and rebuking the ungodly, and patiently *persuading* the sinner to repent; luminous and attractive characteristics of all the examples furnished in apostolic preaching for the salvation of sinners. This gentleman will forever remember his entrance into and departure from the Methodist pulpit in the city of Evansville somewhere near a year ago. So desperate and unlike the manner and matter of the preachings of the apostles in reasoning of "sin, righteousness, and a judgment to come," his denunciation, not so much of sin, as the sinners of Evansville, that it worked a storm of indignation and contempt in disgust and disapprobation from the press and the best class of citizens, generally, and church members, that Mr. Jones became so impressed as to prefer other fields for ministerial performances, and left with unmistakable evidence that his services were not needed in that city. What this renowned devine(?) would have said, had he been contemporaneous with Noah, may be inferred from what he is reported to have said in one of his characteristic sermons on a popular occasion in the year of our Lord 1890. Read the extract ladies and gentlemen of the prohibition faith; read it christians, entitled to the name, read it, and then say what you think such a divine as Sam Jones would have said had he, with his exuberant piety exercised his functions as a divine at the time Noah was found by his son, Ham, naked and drunk in his tent.

The extract says:

Sam Jones is evidently not afraid to let people know where he stands. Hear him: "As a minister of the gospel of Jesus Christ I denounce with all the earnestness of my soul, this awful traffic in human souls, and renounce my allegiance to any party or politics favoring or licensing it; hence I declare I am a concentrated, consolidated, eternal, uncompromising. every day in the year, inside out, stand up and be knocked down prohibitionist; and brethren, I am no more to be blamed for being a prohibitionist than I am to blame for being Sam Jones. I was born the one, and circumstances made me the other. I believe that those who make whisky, those who sell it, the men who rent places where it is to be sold and those who vote for whisky are all going to hell. So help me God. I am for a clean fight every time with their hellish traffic and all the devils in hell cannot shut my mouth on this subject. No man can be a christian unless he votes as he prays."

We remark that such utterances about as nearly represent the history of "Sinbad the Sailor" or the 25th chapter of the "Arabian Nights Entertainment" as the teaching of Christ and his Apostles.

ISAAC.

Next we call attention to Isaac, the illustrious father of Jacob and Esau.

Isaac was one of the patriarchs and next to "Abraham the friend of God" and Isaac's father. The liquor traffic was in existence in the days of the patriarch Isaac and his father, Abraham. The monstrous conception of political prohibition had not had a brain for its agitation and a heart for its impulse up to that day. See Genesis; 27 ch., 25. 27-37v. Where on his dying couch Isaac received *wine* from the hands of his son, Jacob. Said the father, "I will eat of my son's venison that my soul may bless thee," and he brought him *wine* and he *drank*. Then Isaac, the father, said to his son, Jacob, "God give thee the dew of heaven, fatness of the earth, plenty of *corn* and *wine*." At this severe dispensation of Isaac the father, Esau remonstrated, when Isaac answered Esau and said; verse 37: "Behold I have made him thy lord, and all his brethren have I given to him for servants, and with corn and WINE have I sustained him."

How contracted the views, superficial the intelligence and selfish the aims of money-seeking and political aspiring demagogues—itinerant gospel prohibition—men and woman temperance lecturers.

These mercenary beef steak hunters find out the best localities—whose church membership is the largest and wealthiest, as choice fields for benevolent service. They are well known to the lecturing brother and sisterhood, as auguring the most gratifying returns in financial compensation.

In Genesis, 43-34, we have these words, "But Benjamin's mess was five times so much as any of theirs. And they drunk, and were merry." The fluid drunk—we presume was wine or some other intoxicant, as it made them merry. This event was 1707 years before Christ.

Whether or not it would have been, or was lawful for Aaron and his sons to use wine and strong drink temperately; on other occasions, except when engaged in the official devotional services of the tabernacle, the record is silent. It is probable the obligation of abstinence was continuous, as the character of the priesthood should be beyond liability to become intoxicated at any time. The point is clear however, that intoxicants were in use in the days of Aaron and his sons.

Next we have allusion to the cultivation of the grape. 25 ch., 3-4 v. say: "Six years shalt thou sow thy field, and six years shalt thou prune thy vineyard, and gather in the fruit thereof; but on the seventh year shall be a Sabbath of rest to the land; a Sabbath for the Lord; thou shalt neither sow thy field, nor prune thy vineyard."

In this statute there is no prohibition on the seventh year to cultivate the grape, any more than the cultivation of any other growth of the field. There was then no interdiction of the use of the grape excepting for the purpose mentioned, which had no connection with the object of modern prohibitionists. 23 ch, 13 v, says: "And the drink offering thereof shall be of *wine*." 1,490 years before *Christ*.

EXODUS.

Is the next book to Genesis. In the 29 ch, 40 v, these directions in divine service occur: "And with the one lamb thou shalt offer in the morning, one fourth part of a hin of wine for a drink offering." In this case, wine was a part of sacrificial service. Wine then was in use, as in the days of Christ and employed in the devotion to Almighty God.

LEVITICUS.

In the 10 ch of Leviticus, the obligation of the priesthood is distinctly enunciated; 8th verse says, "and the Lord spoke unto Aaron, saying: ' "Do not drink wine nor strong drink, thou nor thy sons with thee, *when* ye go into the *tabernacle* of the congregation lest ye die." ' Drunkenness is odious in any one but especially it must not be indulged in by ministers of sacred service, hence emphatically forbidden to Aaron and his sons.

NUMBERS.

Is the next book of the Old Testament, chapter 6, verses 2-5, you have these words directly from Jehovah to Moses, "Speak unto the children of Isreal and say unto them, when either man or woman shall separate themselves to vow a vow of a Nazarite to separate themselves unto the Lord, he shall separate himself from *wine* and *strong drink* and shall drink no vineagar of wine, or strong drink, neither shall he drink any *liquor* of grapes, nor eat *moist* grapes or *dried*. All the days of his separation shall he eat nothing that is made of the vine tree from the kernals even to the husk. All the days of the vow of his separation there shall no razor come upon his head until the days be fulfilled in which he separateth himself unto the Lord, he shall be holy, and shall let the locks of the hair of his head grow &c."

In this divine enactment observe first that the obligation of *total* abstinence from every substance that might possibly produce inebriation, whether of wine, the vinegar of wine—which means fully *fermented* wine; strong drink—an inflamatory compound made in imitation of grape wine, of dates, figs, honey, etc., of a ready intoxicating effect, a popular beverage used excessively in idolatrous worship, here forbidden only to a Nazarite, and no more peremptorily forbidden than to indulge in the use of dried grapes, the kernals and husks of the vine tree, the razor upon the beard, or scissors upon the locks, or the hair of the head. Secondly this temperance obligation was voluntarily assumed, the men and women signing such pledge did it from choice, not from compulsion. Its application was to themselves and none others. Thirdly, it was not of perpetual obligation, the pledge of total abstinence could be violated at pleasure, but it forfeited the character of the Nazarite that did it, just as the sober man forfeits his character for sobriety the moment he allows intoxication to prostrate his manhood. Without further elaboration, is it not certain that intoxicants existed in the time of Moses, and that there was then, no statute forbidding their temperate use?

See 6 ch. 15 v. and 15 ch. 7-10-24 v. where *wine* is required for a drink offering. Next, observe in the 28th ch. that this drink offering of *wine* was not what prohibitionists will say was the fermented juice of the grape, but possessed intoxicating qualities. 7 verse says, "And the drink offering thereof shall be a fourth part of a hin for one lamb. In the holy place shalt thou cause the STRONG *wine* to be poured unto the Lord for a drink offering."

We confess to a lack of capacity to determine whether it is ignorance or a cheaper grade of deficiency that preponderates in that class of men claiming to be called of God, to preach his truth, that are everlastingly lamenting the misfortune of the church, that it is compelled to use the sacramental cup, sparkling with fermented wine, when the fact is the juice of the grape without fermentation, such as Christ used and made of water, is no wine at all. The best scholarship of the 19th century, enjoying linguistic diplomacy, in answer to the question as to his opinion of the chemical condition of the wine used by Christ at the last supper, said: "Unfermented wine·is fermented nonsense."

Christianity is not a myth, nor the christian scriptures a falsehood. And the piety of the modern pulpit, or pew, that undertakes to improve upon the pattern given from the Mount, and its illustration from the Garden of Eden to the Isle of Patmos would be too pharasaical to merit respectful consideration, much less the commendation its ignorance, vanity and presumption demand.

DEUTERONOMY.

32 ch, 38 v, records the existence of wine as far back as 1451 before Christ. The sons of the faithful were both gluttons and drunkards—see 21 ch, 20-21 v, for which offence God required them to be stoned to death. The rotten sentiment that finds expression in the prayers of the pulpit for murderers in prison cells, and upon the gallows; in the laxity of christian morals at the present day, had no countenance from the great God in the administration of Moses.— 29 ch, read this chapter from 10 to 29. The many ways in which men and women disregard the law of God are recited, and God's method of dealing with offenders. Among other ways to sin was to add "drunkeness to thirst," v 19. *Law*, and not fanaticism, was the order then.

PROHIBITION A FALLACY.

We respectfully ask the attention of the modern pulpit, pew, and the "Women's Temperance Christian Association" especially the scholarly, philanthropic, and we would like to say the motherly attention of *Miss* Susan B. Anthony (she was recently elected to the presidency of the above named organization) to the following interview of the great God with his vicegerent, Moses.—Deuteronomy 14 ch, from 23 to 26 verse: "And thou shalt eat before the Lord thy God, in the place he shall choose to place his name there, the tithe of thy corn, of thy *wine* and of thine oil, and the firstlings of thy herds and thy flocks, that thou mayest learn to fear the Lord thy God always. And if the way be too long for thee, so that thou art not able to carry it, or if the place be too far for thee, which the Lord thy God shall choose to set his name there—when the Lord thy God has blessed thee, then thou shalt turn it into *money*, and bind up the money in thy hand, and shalt go into the place which the Lord thy God shall choose, and thou shalt bestow that money for *whatsoever* thy soul lusteth after, for oxen, or for sheep, or for *wine*, or for STRONG DRINK, or for whatsoever thy soul desireth, and thou shalt eat there before the Lord thy God, and thou shalt rejoice, thou and thy household."

The great principles of personal independence and responsibility, based upon an intelligence that the God of the universe recognized as worthy of his attention and approval were never repealed by the Lord Jesus Christ, nor his inspired apostles. So we conclude that modern legal prohibition is a monster of such hideous mien, "that, to be hated, is but to be seen." There is nothing of God, humanity, civilization, christianity, common sense, nor any other quality of law or ethics to commend it to the approval of any one. Deuteronomy 15 ch, 10-14 v, has an item as to the existence of wine and its uses 1451 years before Christ. 7 ch, 13 v, says: "He (God) will also bless the fruit of thy womb, and the fruit of thy land, thy corn and thy *wine*" &c.

It is not complimentary to the modern pulpit but condemnatory of it, and all its allies of prohibition advocates, whether they appear in Women's Christian Temperance organizations—headed as president of the association by *Miss* Susan B. Anthony, or any other politically interested agencies, to express an ignorant contempt for God's administration of his own affairs, for the welfare of his own people, whose devotion to God was equal, if not superior to the qualities of the *Christian Churches* of the latter part of the 19th century. The idea that human legislation must come to the relief of the sacramental service of the christian churches, advertises the impotency and imbecility of the modern pulpit and its adjuncts.

JUDGES.

In this book, 13 ch, 4, 7, 14 verses, &c: "Therefore I pray thee drink not *wine* nor *strong* drink." This event was 1161 years before Christ. No legal prohibition then. Divine authority was the rule at that time.

RUTH,

Comes next, and the only transaction of *drinking*—whether it would intoxicate judge for yourself. The text, 3ch, 7 v, says: "When Boaz had eaten and *drunk* his heart was merry, &c.

1st SAMUEL.

Is the next book to Ruth. 1st ch, 24 v is a wonderful use of *wine*, especially as it was an integral in the dedication of her son, Samuel, to the service of the God of Isreal. It is worth more than the time for the reader at convenience to turn to this chapter and read it all. Next we quote from 10 ch, 3 v. "Then shalt thou go on forward from thence, and thou shalt come to the plain of Tabor and there shall meet thee three men going up to God to Bethel. One carrying three kids, another carrying three loaves of bread and another carrying a bottle of WINE." Read the whole chapter. See 16-20: "And Jessie took a bottle of *wine* and a kid and sent them by David unto Saul." Wonder what Iowa prohibitionists think of such depravity as here cited, or of such apostates from christianity as instituted a prohibitory law forbidding the juice of grapes, or even cider for family use.

Prohibition and phariseeism were without quotation marks in the prices current circular of fanaticism in days of Jesse, David and Saul. Iowa, Kansas and the Saints of Maine were subsilentio at that remote period. I now call attention to the existence of intoxicants in the days of David, 25 ch, 18 v: "Then Abigail made haste and took two hundred loaves and *two* bottles of *wine* and five sheep already dressed and five measures of parched corn and a hundred clusters of raisins and two hundred cakes of figs, &c." 36 v, and Abigail came to Nabal and behold he held a feast in his house like the feast of a king. And Nabal's heart was merry within him, for he was very *drunken*. Here is the existence of intoxicants directly under the eye of David. It is of no importance whether or not he approved or condemned it. He accepted the result of Nabal's excessive use of intoxicants for which God killed him, and Abigail became David's wife. Will the reader turn to the 25 ch, and read from the 38 to 40 v, which gives in detail the whole transaction how Nabal lost his life and David became the husband of Abigail, Nabal's wife.

2nd SAMUEL.

See 10 ch, 28 v. We will only quote the verse. "Now Absalom had commanded his servants, saying, mark ye now when Amnon's heart is merry with *wine*. No prohibition then, notwithstanding David was upon the throne. We have already quoted, and commented upon 16 ch, 1-2 v.

1st KINGS.

901 years before Christ in 1st Kings, 20 ch, 16-20 v, we have an exhibit of distinguished guests reminding one of what happens at the present day, notably at the Great Capital of our country, Washington City, D. C.

16 v says: "And they went out at noon, but Benhadad was *drinking* himself *drunk* in the pavillion, (modernly called *Shoreham Flats*) he and the kings, the thirty and two kings that helped him." In the 4 ch, 20 v, we have these words 1014 years before Christ: "Judah and Isreal were many, as the sand which is by the sea in multitudes, eating and *drinking* and making *merry*. Possibly it was water or prohibition sweet wine that made them merry! such as the Women's Temperance Christian Association are demanding for sacramental use. Miss Susan B. Anthony's judgment in the premises will be satisfactory if disposed to depose on the premises.

2nd KINGS.

18 ch, 32 v, 710 years before Christ: "A land of corn and *wine*, a land of bread and vineyards, a land of oil and honey, &c." Read the whole chapter.

1st CHRONICLES.

In the 9 ch, 29 v, 1441 before Christ you can read these words: "Some of them were appointed to oversee the vessels and all the instruments of the sanctuary and the fine flour and the *wine* and the oil and the frankincense." 1048 years before Christ Isreal under the eye of David had a jubilee. See 12 ch, 40 v, which reads: "Moreover they that were nigh them brought bread on asses, and on camels and on mules and on oxen, and meat, meal, cakes of figs, and bunches of raisins, and *wine* and oil, and oxen, and sheep abundantly, for there was joy in Isreal." At this great feast and jubilation they were from all the region round-about, and from Issachor, from Zebulan, and from Naphtali." This occasion brings to mind vividly, the grand celebration of the inauguration to the presidency of the American States, at its centennial in New York—April—a year ago, of the illustrious Gen. George Washington, an account of whose travels from his Mt. Vernon homestead, details the fact—of the blending of wine or beer in his palatal demands at every meal. Yet no shadow of intoxication ever darkened the foot way of his travel from the embraces of domestic comfort to the executive chair as the official in chief of the United States of America.

4ch, 20 v, you have these words: "Judah and Isreal were many, as the sand by the sea in multitudes, eating and drinking and making merry." Prohibitionists are all christians and believe the book of inspiration teaches the truth in all things. At this point I wish to call the attention of my distinguished relation, the Rev. John B. English, whose name and mine are the same. His father and mine were brothers, of the same father and mother parentage, hence he is my own dear cousin. In the name I am complimented because of his distinction as a man of letters, sound morality and christian sentiment and ecclesiastical prominence as a D. D. in the ministry of the Baptist church of the United States of America. Doubtless he has honored his call to preach the gospel, in the estimation of Baptists,— and they are almost legion. But like all other good and great men—Adam not excepted, he has blundered frightfully in his conceptions that modern prohibition temperance is an indispensible attribute of christianity. I am led to my ideas of his faith by the following which I copy from the "Voice," a prohibition temperance paper. Read the extract:

DR. BROOKS AT MONTCLAIR FRIDAY EVENING.

Dr. John A. Brooks, prohibition candidate for Vice-President, and Dr. J. B. English of Baltimore, will speak at Montclair, N. J., Friday evening, Oct. 5. Every voter in Dr. English's church, the Grace Baptist, is a party prohibitionist.

I have heard Dr. Brooks talk on prohibition when a candidate for Vice-President. Christ was entertained by the talk of the devil, and I was pleased greatly in listening to Dr. Brooks. Not that he was a devil, or anything thereunto pertaining, but I regreted the fact that a great and good man, as I considered Dr. Brooks to be. could be, by good motives but erronerous convictions brought down so low in sentiment and emotion to presume to advocate the unscriptural, fanatical, not to say the absurd doctrine of prohibition. Dr. English in preaching prohibition is doubtless meeting the obligation of his convictions, but is not nearer meeting the demand of his calling than Eve when she departed from the divine will in wishing to "know good from evil," and deliberately departed from the plain instructions of her Creator. Preach the gospel my dear relative with all your might, but whenever you tincture with political prohibition you put a spider in the gospel pie. The fact that every member of your [the Grace Baptist] Church, is a prohibitionist, does not authorize you to preach prohibition as any part of the gospel of the Lord Jesus Christ. Moreover statutory prohibition is all politics. There is no politics in the gospel of Jesus Christ. Quit it, and honor your calling by preaching "*temperance*, righteousness and a judgment to come."

We further direct my distinguished relative and Dr. Brooks to the 27 c, 27 v, which says: "And over the vineyard was Shimei, the Ramathite, over the increase of the vineyards for the *wine* cellars, Zabdi the Shipmite." Also in the 29c, 21-22 v: "And they sacraficed sacrafices unto the Lord, and offered burnt offerings unto the Lord, even a thousand bullocks, a thousand rams, and a thousand lambs with their *drink* offerings in abundance for *all* Isreal, and did eat and *drink* before the Lord on that day. And they made Solomon, the son of David, King the second time, and annointed him unto the Lord to be the chief governor, and Zadok to be priest."

2nd CHRONICLES.

Read 2 ch, 15 v: "Now therefore the wheat, and the barley, the oil, and the *wine* which my Lord hath spoken of, let him send unto my servants." 11 ch, 11 v, says: "And he fortified the strongholds, and put captains in them, and stores of victuals, and of oil and *wine*."

Prohibitionists will say, prohibition, local option, total abstinence, and only drug store saloons had a poor showing during the reign of the wisest king that ever had the divinely approved official oversight of God's people, Isreal.

EZRA AND NEHEMIAH.

Ezra is silent. It is a book of reminescences, reciting historical events. But it is worth the reader's time to examine the book of Nehemiah, giving at length, the existence and use of wine.

2 ch, 1 v, says: "It came to pass in the twentieth year of Artaxerxes, the king, that *wine* was before him, and I took up the wine and gave it unto the

king." See 5 ch, 15 v. The 17 -18 vs read: "Moreover there were at my table a hundred and fifty Jews and rulers, besides those that came in unto us from among the heathens that are about us, and that which was prepared for me daily was one ox and six choice sheep; also, fowls were for me, and once in ten days store of *all sorts of wine*."

One of the ablest commentators to be found in the galaxy of ecclesiastical celebrities furnishes the following portrait of this, among the greatest of Bible characters, omitting only the Great God and Jesus Christ the Saviour. This limneric brush hands you the following portrait of Nehemiah: "In him we have the shining character of an able governor, and true patriot, deeply concerned for the good of his country and the honor of religion, choosing to leave an honorable and profitable post in the greatest court in the world, and generously spending the riches he had gained in it for the public benefit of his fellow Isrealites."

It is not to be wondered at that there is no prohibition sentiment among the Jews, their Bible (the Old Testament) does not authorize it in precept nor example, and is not a fact while they all drink with exceptions, yet, even business sobriety characterize them as a universal nationality. They all remember Nehemiah, and like good living.

In addition to these utterances please see ch 5, v 11, "Restore I pray you, to them, even this day, their land, their *vineyards*, their olive yards, and their houses, ALSO the hundredth part of the money, and of the corn, the *wine* that ye exact of them." See 10 ch 37 v, 13 ch, 5-12 v, especially observe 15 v, which reads: "In those days saw I, in Judah, some treading wine presses on the Sabbath, and bringing in sheaves and lading asses, as also wine, grapes and figs &c. It was the desecration of the Sabbath and not the wine &c they carried to market at which the complaint is alleged.

An inadvertance caused us to overlook 6 ch, 9 v, in Ezra which reads: "And that which they have need of, both young bullocks, and rams, and lambs, for the burnt offerings of the God of heaven, wheat, salt, *wine*, and oil, according to the appointment of the priests which are at Jerusalem, let it be given them day by day without fail." Any prohibition, local option, or total abstinence then, do you think?

7 ch, 20-23 v, verse 21 says- "And I, even Artaxerxes, the king, do make a decree to all the *treasurers* which are beyond the river, that whatsoever Ezra, the priest, the scribe of the law of the God of heaven shall require of you it shall be done speedily." 22 v: "Unto a hundred talents of silver, and to a hundred measures of wheat, and to a *hundred baths* of *wine*, and to a hundred baths of oil and salt without measuring how much." 23 v: "Whatsoever is commanded by the God of heaven let it be dilligently done for the house of the God of heaven." Do prohibition christians give it up that the Jewish dispensation could worship the infinite to acceptance without the aid of the civil law, and that prohibition was not a demand in that dispensation?

MELCHISEDEC and ABRAHAM.

As far ago as the time of Melchisedec and Abram subsequently called, "Abraham the friend of God," nearly 2,000 years before the birth of the redeeming God—Jesus Christ, these words are recorded. Genesis 14 ch, 18 v. "And Melchisedec, King of Salem, brought forth bread and *wine*, and he was the priest of the most high God. And he blessed him and said and blessed be Abraham of the most high God, possessor of heaven and earth; and blessed be the most high God which hath delivered thine enemies into thy hands." According to learned commentators, this offering of bread and wine was simply a banquet to Abraham and his soldiery, for their gallantry and triumph, of humanity over brutality in their rescue of Lot, the nephew of Abraham, the women and goods and people held in captivity by Chedorlaomer, king of Sodom and Gomorrah. Of this king of Salem, priest of the most high God, a man of official renown, of consummate righteousness—as God's servant—the idea that such a man of such distinction—personally and officially four thousand years ago—should have perpetrated so grave an offence as to offer a bakuet of "bread and wine" to such a captain and his soldiery as Abraham. the friend of God, in token of esteem, and to invigorate his mind and body is enough to cause all prohibitionists to howl like hounds in the chase at the sound of a huntsman's bugle. Is it possible that such depravity should have existed two thousand years before Christ and that such characters as Abraham and Melchisedec should have been central figures in the scene? None but prohibitionists need answer this inquiry.

The reader at his leisure, is requested to turn to Hebrews in the New Testament where St. Paul recites this transaction with elaboration and perspicuity, so that the events recorded in Genesis are recognized by apostolic inspiration, as verities and reliable authority that the banquet of bread and wine given to Abraham and his soldiers by Melchisedec was a transaction under the eye and with the approval of the Great God Himself.

In Genesis, 49ch, 11 v, reads: "Binding his fold to the vine and his ass's colt unto the choice vine, he washed his garments in *wine* and his clothes in the blood of grapes. And his eyes shall be red with *wine* and his teeth white with milk." A celebrated commentator, Joseph Benson, well known to the Methodist Ministry especially, holds these words in verse 11: "It is here foretold that the tribe of Judah should inhabit a fruitful land, and especially it should abouud with milk and *wine*, that vines should be so *common* and so *strong* that they should tie their asses to them, and so fruitful that they should load their asses from them, *wine* being as plentiful as *water*, so that the men of that tribe should be very healthful and lively, their eyes *brisk* and *sparkling*, and their teeth white. In Christ there is plenty of all that is *nourishing* and *refresh ing* to the soul, and which maintains and cheers the divine life. In it, in Him, we have *wine* and milk, the riches of Judah's tribe without money and without price." In this event we have something that transpired nearly 1700 before Christ. Temperance prohibition was born of ignorance and has no claim upon the respect of intelligence.

ESTHER.

Is the next book we notice. The novel is yet to be written that will have the entertainment in the broad field of imagination and romance, with or without duplication in reality, that will equal this wonderful production of sacred reminiscence. It is worth far more than the price of the small volume to every Jew, especially, or Christian, to have him furnished with the following comment on the history of that wonderful woman, Esther. In this book we are told "how Esther came to be queen, and Mordecai to be great at Court, how Haman obtained an order for the destruction of the Jews, the distress of the Jews, the defeat of Haman's plot against Mordecai, the defeating of his plot against the Jews etc. The whole scheme failed to accomplish its purpose by the providential appearance on the scene of "one woman" whose name was Esther, a Jewish captive, who, for her remarkable beauty, was espoused to Ahasueris and raised to the throne of Persia, and by her extraordinary interest in the king, rescued the Jewish nation from a general massacre, to which they were appointed by Haman, one of the king's favorites. This sacred record shows the peculiar care of God over those Isrealites scattered abroad among the heathen, and manifests that the eye of a watchful providence is constantly superintending all nations, by which the aspirings of the greatest men are often curbed and broken, wicked designs blasted, piety and virtue protected, and God declared to be the almighty defender of good men, and of the true religion in all ages and generations." We now ask the christian reader's attention to what the book of Esther has to say on the question of intoxicants.

Chapter 1. 7 v: "And they gave them drink in vessels of gold, (the vessels being diverse one from another) and royal *wine* in *abundance*, according to the state of the king, and the drinking was according to the law; none did compel, for the king had appointed to all the officers of his house that they should do according to every man's pleasure." 10 v: "On the seventh day when the heart of the king was merry with *wine* &c, &c." 5 ch, 6 v: "And the king said unto Esther at the banquet of *wine* &c, &c." 7 ch, 2 v: "And the king said again unto Esther, on the second day of the banquet of *wine* &c, &c."

THE BOOK OF JOB.

We will now present for consideration what he has said on the subject of intoxicants; one of the most distinguished and reliable characters mentioned in the Old Testament Scriptures. In the book of Job 1 chapter it begins: "There was a man in the land of Uz, whose name was Job, and that man was perfect and upright and one that feared God and eschewed evil." This man was not a crank, a debauch, and libertine, nor prohibitionist. 2nd verse: "There were born unto him seven sons and three daughters. His substance also, was seven thousand sheep, and three thousand camels, and five hundred yoke of oxen, and five hundred she asses, and a very great household, so that this man was the greatest of all the men of the East." This wonderful agriculturalist flourished as far back as Abraham. He was a pattern of fixed and solid piety, all his utterances are magnificent and profound, his language is poetical, dramatical and beautiful, no matter of what subject he treats, nor the occassion of his sublime utterances, his integrity, his unswerving devotion and unfaltering trust in God gives him a sublimity of charrcter never excelled in bible reminescences. According to the Prophet Ezekiel 14-14, he ranked with Noah and Daniel, and the Apostle James places him an octave higher in moral grandner and spiritual purity and fidelity than all his contemporaries, predecessors or successors in the galaxy of great and holy men. Is it possible that such a man had his day in the reign of intoxicants, or that intoxicants were in reach in his day. In 1 ch. 4 v. it is said: "His sons went and feasted in their houses, every one his day (birthday) and sent and called for their three sisters to eat and *drink* with them." As to the nature of the fluid drank verse 13 says: "There was a day when his sons and daughters were eating, and drinking *wine*, in their eldest brother's house." Wine, then, was the fluid drank."

It is a fact then, that intoxicants had their use in the days of one of the most inveterate devotees of devotion to God, and unswerving consecration of his whole manhood and life to his reveald manifestations. Prohibition temperance lecturers, whether St. John, General Fisk, or all the smaller lights, only advertize their utter ignorance of the divine character of his administration in attempts to auction their ignorance to fanatical bidders in exchange, if they could, for political offices or financial gain.

In the 18th verse: "Thy sons and thy daughters were eating and drinking *wine* in their eldest brother's house." We use these utterances to show that *wine* was used by men and women in the days, of Job, one of the holiest and wisest men that ever lived. We now direct attention to 12 ch, 25 v. I will only quote the text in point, omitting the circumstances that led to it. "They grope in the dark without light, and he (God) maketh them to stagger like drunken men." Then it is a fact that Jehovah himself was advised that drunkenness had its subjects in the days of Job, and that no suggestion is intimated, either by the illustrious patriarch or the Great God himself, that, to prevent it, local option, total abstinence or prohibition, by human statutes should be interposed.

PSALMS.

The next book to Job is the book of Psalms. Of its author and authors, the distinguished commentator, well known to all Methodist ministers, especially, the linguist, Joseph Benson, says: "We have now before us one of the choicest parts of the Old Testament, wherein there is so much of Christ and his gospel, as well as God and his law, that it has been called the summary of both Testaments. This book has been always held in greatest veneration. Dr. Horne in his commentary says: They are an epitome of the bible, adapted to the purposes of devotion. St. Bassil says it is a complete body of divinity. The distinguished historian and commentator, Dr. Horne, further says: "They treat occassionally of the creation and formation of the world, the dispensation of providence, and the economy of grace, the transactions of patriarchs, the exodus of the children of Isreal, their journey through the wilderness, and settlement in Canaan, their law, priesthood, and ritual. the exploits of their great men wrought through faith, the sufferings and victories of David, the peaceful and happy reign of Solomon, the advent of Messiah, his incarnation, birth, life, death, resurrection and ascension, kingdom and priesthood,. the effusion of the spirit, the conversion of the nations, the rejection of the Jews, the establishment and of increase. and perpetuity of the christian church, the end of the world, general judgment, the condemnation of the wicked, and the final triumph of the righteous with their Lord and King.

The character of such testimony as the Psalms presents ought to find acceptance in the credulity of the pulpit, pew, the choir, Women's Temperance Christian Association, prohibition, gospel temperance lecturers throughout Iowa, Kansas, Maine, and all Christendom. What then is recorded in the Psalms on the subject of intoxicants? The first mention of the inebriating extract of the grape can be found in 4 ch, 11 v, which says: "Thou hast put gladness in my heart, more than in the time that their corn and *wine* increased." 60 ch. 3 v, these words occur: "Thou hast made us to drink the *wine* of astonishment." 75, 8: "For in the land of the Lord there is a cup and the wine is red." 78 ch, 65 v: "Then the Lord awaked as one out of sleep, like a mighty man that *shouteth* by reason of *wine*." 104 ch, 14-15 vs: "He (God) causeth the grass to grow for cattle, and herb for the service of man, and *wine* that maketh *glad* the heart of man." 107 ch, 27 v: "They reel to and fro and stagger like a drunken man." 68 ch, 12 v: "I was made the song of the drunkard."

What does the pious, par-excellent prohibition philantropist have to say to the prevalence of the intoxicating liquid in the days of the Psalmists, including David, Moses, Asaph, and others who praised God rapturously in Psalms, hymns, and spiritual songs at a period when intoxicating beverages were often indulged in to excess, with no effort for civil legislation to prevent it.

The purity of the motive and the sincerity of the purpose of prohibitionists are not called in question. A higher authority than St. John and Gen. Fisk and prohibition temperance lecturers generally, and the Woman's Christian Temperance Union, with Miss Susan B. Anthony as its president added, must have something more than *sentiment* to enforce respect for their demand for statutory legislation to abate the existence of intoxicants. If the Bible and constitutional law be wanting to authorize their demands, such demands are not entitled to respect.

DAVID.

David, the Hebrew bard, and as he is spoken of by all the pulpit as the sweet singer in Isreal. David was not obnoxious to the moral law, as an inebriate, nor was his moral escutcheon tarnished with any offence of common grade. He enjoyed and deserved immense distinction as one that all Isreal could trust. The signet of divine favor was upon his innocent brow as the award to virtuous fidelity in all contests where temptation offered attractions and exerted its force to swerve him from the rule of personal and official fidelity to law. He was the grand center of confidence, and doubt as to his departure from the white lines of any personal acts infracting the rights of any of his subjects as the chief official of the commonwealth of Isreal, was without a heart to conceive the possibility of such an apostacy. Nevertheless the time and circumstances to test his merit arose, and his susceptibility to show himself mortal appears in that he was under temptation, susceptible of the sin of covetousness, which according to the teaching of Christ and his Apostles, is a great sin, though mild in form is disastrous and damnable in results. Well, David observed on a circumstantial occasion that a prominent subject of his reign possessed property of singular qualities of value to him personally, and he had a desire to possess it; and like many distinguished officials, well known to the reading public of the United States, he succumbed to the blandishments of the scene, and sacrificed all that was noble, and great and pure in his personal and official character to the achievment of his base desire, and became an adulterer and murderer. Angels fell, Adam and Eve kept not their first estate, and David descended, almost in a moment, to the profoundest depths of horrible depravity. Had this distinguished servant of God, the pebble from whose sling in boyhood, at a time of Isreal's extremity, he sent with unerring aim a fatal touch to the brow of the insolent, God defying and Isreal hating Goliah of Gath, been the subject of a draft of intoxicants from a high license saloon or a pious drug store, his infraction of personal and official purity would have been thundered and echoed in every prohibition lecture from the birth of its monstrosity to present time. The divine clemency that can possibly save a drunkard or saloon-keeper, or anyone else soever engaged in the liquor traffic from the perdition to which, in the judgment of prohibitionists, their depravity consigns them, was available in David's case. And a repentance unto life and a subsequent reformation from the hour the consuming fires of his guilt by the the sweet waters of forgiveness were quenched, to the hour of his farewell song, I am going home, his character and the greatness of his mind and heart for the honor of God and the happiness of every man, woman and child stand out like the mountain—higher than the clouds, and as broad as the boundary lines of human existence, solid, and as imperishable as the granite foundation on which time was built.

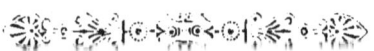

PROVERBS.

Its authorship is that of Solomon, who according to Joseph Benson, one of the clearest, most comprehensive writers that has ever written a commentary on the Old and New testaments. Of Solomon this author says: "He was used by the Holy Ghost for making known the *mind* of God to us. He was endued with an uncommon share of wisdom, and was a great author. He spoke of the cedars of Lebanon, unto the hyssop that springeth out of the wall. He spoke of beasts and of fowls and creeping things, and of fishes. His proverbs were the dictates of the spirit of God in Solomon. We have no book so serviceable for the right ordering of our conversations as Solomon's proverbs, containing in a little compass a complete body of divine ethics, politics and economics, exposing every vice, recommending every virtue, and suggesting rules for the government of ourselves in every relation and condition, and every turn of conversation." Certainly such a character will command attention from prohibitionists. What then was the state of society in his eventful days as king of Isreal? 4ch. 17 v. speaking of the wicked days: "They drink the *wine* of violence." Then there was no prohibition at that time, 1,000 years before Christ. Speaking of wisdom, he says, 9 ch. 2 v: "She hath killed her beasts; she hath mingled her *wine*; she also, hath furnished her table." 5 v: "Come eat of my bread, and *drink* of the *wine* which I have *mingled*."

20 ch. 1 v. "Wine is a mocker and strong drink is raging, and whosoever is deceived thereby is not wise." A celebrated commentator on these words says: "wine immoderately drank makes men mockers or scoffers at God and men." No excuse can be offered for excessive indulgence in "wine or strong drink," any more than to indulge the vitiated qualities of covetousness, adultery or fornication. But for any or all immoral habits, statutory enactment is not the remedy according to the condition of the body politic during the reign, of this chief officer of the commonwealth of Isreal—as king and successor of David and the wisest man that ever lived. Yet, nothing is recorded in his administration remotely suggesting laws of force to prevent the possibility of the inexcusable and reprehensible use of "*wine* and

strong drink" to excess. 3 ch, 9-10v: "Honor the Lord with thy substance, so shall thy barns be filled with plenty and thy presses shall burst out with new wine." 23 ch, 20-21 v: "Be not among wine bibbers, among riotous eaters of flesh, for the *drunkard* and the glutton shall come to poverty." This is sound temperance talk but not prohibition.

31 ch, 4-5 v: "It is not for Kings O Lemuel, it is not for kings to drink wine, nor for prince's strong drink, lest they drink and forget the law and pervert the judgment of any of the afflicted.

6 v: "Give strong drink unto him that is ready to perish and wine unto those that be of heavy hearts."

7 v: "Let him drink and forget his poverty, and remember his misery no more." On these verses, our Commentator holds the following comment: "It is not for kings to drink wine—namely to *excess*, as the next verse explains it: lest they drink and forget the law. The laws of God by which they are to *govern themselves* and their kingdoms, and pervert the judgment of the afflicted—Which may be easily done by a drunken judge, because drunkenness deprives a man of the use of his reason, by which

alone men can distinguish between right and wrong, and withal stirs up those passions in him which incline both to precipitation and partiality. "Give strong drink unto him that is ready to perish"— to faint—for such need a cordial.

Let him drink and forget his poverty—for wine moderately used allays men's cares and fears and cheers the spirits."

26ch. 9 v: "As a thorn goeth up into the hands of a drunkard, so is a parable in the mouth of fools."

It is obvious from the premises that political inhibition was unknown to Solomon.

ECCLESIASTES.

This book is next to Proverbs. Commentors say "it was designed to describe men's true happiness, and the way leading to it." The son of David King Solomon, was its author, therefore canonical. 2 ch, 24v, says: "There is nothing better for a man than that he should eat and drink, and he should make his soul enjoy good in his labour. This also I saw was from God." We presume the eating and drinking as to its nature was altogether a matter of taste and rational convictions, as to what he should eat and drink. This is the original platform on which the human race was commenced, and God has never ordered its amendment or repeal by human legislation. And the man or men, who have forfeited and dishonored the high and divinely approved preogative in the gift of his manhood as to become an habitual inebriate, should by statutory legislation be denied the right of franchise, as well as punished for a voluntary disability and unfitness for the high relations to society, to law. and God; of honoring the preogative and obligation of an intelligent, sober, sovereign elector in the creation of laws for the government of men.

9th ch. 7 v. "Go thy way, eat thy bread with joy and drink thy *wine* with a merry heart, for God now accepteth thy works." This text is only a crumb thrown out as a relish for the Prohibition Whale. 10th ch. 17 v. "Blessed art thou, O land when thy king is the son of nobles, and thy princes eat in due season, for strength and not for drunkenness!" 19 v. "A feast is made for laughter, and *wine* maketh merry, but money answereth all things." Here is the origin of trusts.

3d ch. 13 v. "And every man should eat and drink, and enjoy the good of all his labour."

5th ch., 18 v. "Behold it is good and comely for one to eat and drink, and to enjoy the good of all his labour all the days of his life which God giveth him; for it is his portion." Surely no such a law as modern prohibitionests seek had been enacted at this period.

8th ch., 15 v. "Then I commanded mirth, because a man hath no better thing under the the sun, than to eat and *drink*, and be merry; for that shall abide with him of his labour all the days of his life which God giveth him under the sun."

The SONGS of SOLOMON.

This book, commentators agree that, it is to describe the mutual love, union and communion, which is between Christ and his church in the various conditions to which it is liable in this world.

1 ch, 2 v: "For thy love is better than *wine*," 4 v: "We will remember thy love more than *wine*."

ISAIAH.

One authorized to speak, "Thus saith the Lord." One of the most learned and reliable commentators of the Old and New Testament scriptures, has this to say of Isaiah. Prohibitionists, local optionists and total abstainers will accredit as acceptable authority. Our author says: "He was the *prince* of all the prophets. He is esteemed—and most justly the most eloquent of all the prophets. In him we meet with all the purity of the Hebrew tongue. There are more quotations taken out of this book than out of all the other prophets."

"St. Jerome says, "that the instructions they give in morality and divinity, are highly excellent. He describes the true nature of religion in so clear and so strong a manner that this book will be eminently useful to all pious minds in all ages." What then has this prophet to say on the question of intoxicants? Hear him, 1 ch, 22 v: "Thy silver is become dross, thy *wine* mixed with water." Why do not prohibitionists extend their ideas and action and undertake to limit—if they may not paralyze a monster, (trust combines) to which the liquor traffic is as mild as a midsummer sunshine compared to a cyclone against the interest of human want and necessity. What says the 23 v?—"Thy princes are rebellious and companions of *thieves*, every one loveth gifts and followeth after rewards; they judge not the fatherless, neither doth the cause of the widow come unto them." Wonder if prohibitionists understand to what we allude in this quotation? Possibly they do! If not, read entire—the first chapter of Isaiah and they will be correctly advised. Then turn to the 24 ch. and read it all. You will then admit that intoxicants existed in the days of Isaiah. In the 5 ch, 11 v, you have these words: "Woe unto them that rise up early in the morning that they may follow strong drink; that continue until night, till wine inflame them." Such unfortunate men lived in the days of this prophet. The import of the term *woe* is frightful. It carries with it—that there is nothing at the end of such a career but *hell*, with its adjudicated torments. Such total failures of the human race according to the "Book" are doomed to everlasting destruction.

The man or woman that cannot use intoxicants without reaching habitual drunkenness, should be pitied rather than denounced. Greater offenders than drunkards against God's moral law, and the interests of humanity, have been seen in the house of devotion. The money glutton; Judas, was one of the "chosen twelve" whose successors today, can be counted by the thousands. Yet the pulpit extends to their hypocritical lips the sacramental cup. Judas met the fate his perfidy provoked, and, the jury that lessens the penalty to the accused because he was drunk when he committed the offence, is a disgrace to the jury panel. God's law allows no such apology. "The wages of sin is death." And the preacher and pew, that retains in membership the man or woman, known to be acceptable to the church only for their money contributions, are disgraceful and degrading to christianity. Law, and not sentiment, is God's method of governing the world.

5 ch, 12 v: "The harp and the viol, the tabor and pipe, and *wine* are in their feasts." 22 ch, 13 v. says, "Behold joy and gladness slaying oxen and killing sheep, eating flesh and drinking *wine.*

24 ch, 6-11 v: "The new wine mourneth, the vine languisheth, all the merry hearted do sigh. They shall not drink *wine* with a song; *strong* drink shall be bitter to them that drink it, there is a crying for

wine in the streets, all joy is darkened, the mirth of the land is gone."

28 ch, 1-7 v: "Woe to the crown of pride, to the *drunkards* of Ephraim, whose glorious beauty is a fading flower which are on the head of them which are *overcome* with *wine*." Can a prohibitionist observe any difference in the conduct of men at that— and the present day? See 29 ch, 9 v, and it will be observed that something else than wine and strong drink make men drunk.

55 ch, 1 v, "Ho, every one that thirsteth, come ye to the waters, and he that hath no money, come ye, buy and eat, yea come buy *wine* and milk, without money and without price.

56 ch, 12 v, "Come ye, say they, I will fetch *wine* and fill ourselves with *strong drink*." 36 ch, 17 v: "I will take you to a land of corn and *wine*; a land of bread and *vineyards*." Wonder if the prophet meant that the land spoken of, was Iowa, Kansas or the sober drug store State of Maine? The president, male or female, of any duly organized "Womans Temperance *Christian* Union," can answer at convenience.

62 ch, 8 v, says: "The Lord has sworn by his

right hand "I will no more give my corn to be meat for thine enemies, and the sons of the strangers shall not drink thy wine, for which thou hast laboured."

In the 65 ch, 8 v, you have this text: "Thus saith the Lord, as you have the new *wine* in the cluster, and one saith, destroy it not, for a blessing is it." Iowa christian prohibitionists can reflect on the import of this text at leisure.

63 ch, 2 v, says "Wherefore art thou red in thine apparel, and thy garments like him that treadeth in the *wine* fat." Read the whole chapter. See 21 ch, 5 v: "Prepare the table, watch in the watchtower, eat, drink, arise, ye princes and annoint the shield, &c." We might quote this prophet further but it is not necessary.

JEREMIAH.

Is before the reader as the next prophet to *Isaiah*. The authority from which we quote says: "He was appointed to the prophetic office from his mother's womb, and began his ministry very young, 629 years before Christ. He was ordained to prophesy, see 1 ch, 5 v, not only to the Jews but to all to whom God sent him.

He uttered prophecies not only against God's chosen people, but against the *Egyptians*, the *Philistines*, the *Moabites*, the *Ammonites*, the *Idumeans*, the *Syrians* and especially against the *Babylonians*. He was sublime and elegant in his utterances. A man of unblemished character, piety and conscientious integrity, a warm lover of his country, whose miseries he pathetically deplores. And he chose rather to abide with them and undergo all hardships in their company, than separately to enjoy a state of ease and plenty which the favour of the King of Babylon would have secured to him."

It is profoundly strange and mortifying, that the modern pulpit fails to utilize—and furnish to the Gentile pew, the facts of the unity of the human race—that God and his government has ever been the same—that human nature has never changed, that disobedience to God's moral law is no worse nor better now than in the days of the prophets. The modern practice of picking out one sin of a thousand and damning it to hell and excusing all the balance, is the reason why infidelity has grown fat and defiant. Such a condition of affairs appeared in the days of Christ and his Apostles, straining out gnats and swallowing camels—literally—straining at gates and swallowing saw-mills. St: Paul leveled the artillery of Heaven against all such sleepers, when he said: "Awake to righteousness and sin not, for some have not the knowledge of God, this I speak to your shame." But what was the state of sobriety in Jeremiah's day? His ministry continued for forty years.

23 ch, 9 v, says: "All my bones shake, I am like a drunken man whom *wine* hath overcome." Then they got drunk by taking too much, as is sometimes the case at Washington City, according to the papers.

35 ch, 2 v: "Go unto the house of the Rechabites and bring them into the house of the Lord, into one of the *chambers* and give them *wine* to drink."

5 v: "And I set before them *pots* full of *wine* and *cups*, and I said unto them, *Drink ye wine*."

6 But they said, We will drink no wine; for Jonadab the son of Rechab our father commanded us, saying, Ye shall drink no wine, *neither* ye, nor your sons for ever:

7 Neither shall ye build house, nor sow seed, nor plant vineyard, nor have *any*: but all your days ye shall dwell in tents; that ye may, live many days in the land where ye *be* strangers.

8 Thus have we obeyed the voice of Jonadab the son of Rechab our father in all that he hath charged us, to drink no wine all our days, we, our wives, our sons, nor our daughters;

9 Nor to build houses for us to dwell in; neither have we vineyard, nor field, nor seed:

10 But we have dwelt in tents, and have obeyed, and done according to all that Jonadab our father commanded us.

11 But it came to pass, when Nebuchadrezzar king of Babylon came up into the land, that we said, Come, and let us go to Jerusalem for fear of the army of the Chaldeans, and for fear of the army of the Syrians: so we dwell at Jerusalem.

12 ¶ Then came the word of the LORD unto Jeremiah, saying,

13 Thus saith the LORD of hosts, the God of Isreal; Go and tell the men of Judah and the inhabitants of Jerusalem, Will ye not receive instruction to hearken to my words? saith the LORD.

14 The words of Jonadab the son of Rechab, that he commanded his sons not to drink wine, are performed; for unto this day they drink none, but obey their father's commandment: notwithstanding I have spoken unto you, rising early and speaking; but ye harkened not unto me.

15 I have sent also unto you all my servants the prophets, rising up early and sending *them*, saying, Return ye now every man from his evil way, and amend your doings, and go not after other gods to serve them, and ye shall dwell in the land which I have given to you and to your fathers: but ye have not inclined your ear, nor harkened unto me.

16 Because the sons of Jonadab the son of Rechab have performed the commandment of their father, which he commanded them; but this people hath not hearkened unto me:

17 Therefore thus saith the LORD God of hosts, the God of Isreal; Behold, I will bring upon Judah and upon all the inhabitants of Jerusalem all the evil that I have pronounced against them: because I have spoken unto them, but they have not heard; and I have called unto them; but they have not answered.

18 ¶ And Jeremiah said unto the house of the Rechabites, Thus saith the LORD of hosts, the God of Isreal; Because ye have obeyed the commandment of Jonadad your father, and kept all his precepts, and done according unto all that he hath commanded you;

19 Therefore thus saith the LORD of hosts, the God of Isreal; Jonadab the son of Rechab shall not want a man to stand before me for ever."

From these utterances of the prophet who expressed distinctly and fully the divine will, we observe here as every where in the Book of Inspiration, that divine and parental authority is not transferred and surrendered to human legislation on questions purely moral in their nature. The temptation to drink wine to drunkenness with all its attractive appliances was resisted because of parental authority, attended with God's approval and blessing.

Only 588 years before Christ this wonderful reprover of wickedness records in the 40 ch, 10 v, these words "I will dwell at Mizpah, but ye, gather ye *wine*, and summer fruits, and oil and put them in your vessels and dwell in your cities that ye have taken."

48 ch, 33 v: "And joy and gladness is taken from the plentiful field and from the land of Moab, and I will have caused *wine* to fail from the *wine* presses. None shall tread with shouting. In all this God is in controversy with wrong doers, then as in the days of Christ. But no prohibition!!!

5 ch. 7 v., says "Babylon has been a golden cup in the Lord's hand, that made all the earth drunken; nations have drunk of her wine; therefore the nations are mad." Prohibitionists of every grade and type, the Woman's *Christian* Temperance Union especially, are left to analyze the import of this text. If all such would read the scriptures and get information as to God's method of governing this world, they would cease to appear as a fading star or a frosted leaf. "My people are destroyed for lack of knowledge" is an accusation against presumption and ignorance.

We omitted by accident our recital from 31 ch. 12 v. which reads: "Therefore they shall come and sing in the height of Zion, and shall flow together to the goodness of the Lord, for wheat, *and for wine*, and for oil, and for the young of the flock, and of the herd, and their souls shall be as a watered garden; and they shall not sorrow any more at all." Political depravity and mercenary aspirations, are plainly seen between the lines in all prohibition movements.

The idea, the fact, that any one, male or *feme nine* should have to come to Jerseyville, or any other locality of its pretentions, intelligence, morality, and christianity, to advance its civilization, with a harrangue on prohibition-temperance, is the acme of rediculousness. The ne plus ultra of superciliousness. And to the extent such agencies are recognized as a necessity to their civil, moral and religious welfare, is but an advertisement of the *idiocy* of the agent coming, the agency sending, or the imbeciles accepting and passing around the hat to meet the expense of their service.

Some birds fail to reach the bush or perch of their roost until nightfall darkens the passage of their flight on the home stretch. So with at least ninety-nine of every one hundred found in the prohibition lecture field, like "Diana of the Ephesians" it is the source of the necessary supplies to keep their ark above the waves of actual want; hence any thing that will pay! And as a sentimental, not a *Bible Christianity* invites their approach, as authorized by prohibitionists, local optionists and total abstainers.

LAMENTATIONS.

Jeremiah is the author of this book.

2 ch. 12 v: "They say unto their mothers, where is corn and wine?" 1 ch. 15 v: "The Lord hath trodden the Virgin, the daughter of Judah as in a *wine* press."

The next prophet is

EZEKIEL.

Of this eminently distinguished prophet, one of the four greater prophets, our commentator says: "His genius led him to amplification, like that of Ovid, Lucan and Juvenal, among the Roman poets; though occasionally he shows himself capable of the austere and concise manner of which the 7 ch. is a remarkable instance. But the divine spirit did not over rule the natural bent of his mind. Variety is thus produced in the sacred writings. Nahum sounds the trupet of war, Hosea is sententious, Isaiah sublime, Jeremiah pathetic, *Ezekiel* copious.

What of the liquor traffic and prohibition during the period he "spake as God commanded him?" *Wine* was then in use as it is to-day. 27 ch, 18 v. says: "Damascus was thy merchant in the multitude of the wares of thy making for the multitude of all riches in the *wine* of Helbon and white wool."

44 ch, 21 v, you read: "Neither shall any priest drink wine when they enter into the inner court." In these quotations it is observed that wine was an item of merchandise, but its use denied to the priests when serving officially in the inner court.

DANIEL

Comes next. The reputation of this prophet is so well known by the ministry and all church people that he needs no commendation from any commentator to command the confidence of any one as to his pretensions as a prophet. 1 ch, 5 v, says: "And the king appointed them a daily provision of the king's meat, and of the *wine* which he *drank*." 8 v: "But Daniel would not defile himself with the portion of the king's meat nor with the *wine* which he drank." It appears that in this case that other motive than the offer of wine was rejected. He refused to accept the king's meat also.

In the 10 ch, 2-3 v, are these remarkable facts: "In those days I, Daniel, was mourning three full weeks. I ate no pleasant bread, neither came flesh nor *wine* in my mouth, &c." The wine, the bread and the flesh are equally the subject of his self denial during his three weeks fast. And it is absolutely certain that this illustrious prophet had not conceived the *sublime* idea of a prohibitory temperance law at that time. Daniel was not merely a historian but Jehovah's inspired prophet, whose teachings on moral and religious questions are as authorative to-day as when first uttered.

The 9 ch, 2-4 v show the existence of wine and winepresses. 14 ch, 7 v. says: "They that dwell under his shadow shall return; they shall revive as the corn and grow as the vine, the scent thereof shall be as the cedar of Lebanon." In the 3 ch, 1 v: "flaggons of wine" are spoken of.

HOSEA

Stands accredited with authority to say, "Thus saith the Lord."

2 ch, 8 v, says: "For she did not know that I gave her corn and *wine* and oil and multiplied her silver and gold which they prepared for Baal. 9 v: "Therefore will I return and take away in the time thereof, and my *wine* in the *season* thereof." Other allusions to wine in this chapter and other matters that have their reproving application to the present time as when they first thundered in the ears of apostacy. Read it!

Read the 4 ch, and it will be perceived that some other violations of God's moral laws are more common at the present day than the offence of intoxication from the excessive use of wine or strong drink. Yet the pulpit and moral lecturers, whether men or women on these violations of divine, and even civil laws, are as still as tomb-stones and as silent as shadows.

7 ch, 5 v: "In the day of our *King* the princes have made him *sick* with *bottles* of wine." Has there nothing of this kind of bribery been going on during the 19th century in the United States?

JOEL.

Is in the group of what are considered the lesser prophets, to whom the "word of the Lord came" 800 years before Christ.

Reliable data says of him: "He is elegant, perspicuous, copious and fluent, sublime, animated and energetic. He foretells the plentiful effusions of the Holy Spirit in the days of Christ." On the question of intoxicants, he has this to say, 1 ch, 5 v: "Awake ye *drunkards and weep;* and *howl* all ye drinkers of wine, because of the new wine, because it is cut off from your mouth." No prohibition then, but temperance strongly demanded, and drunkenness severely denounced.

10 v: "The land mourneth, the corn is wasted, the new wine is dried up, the oil languisheth." 11 v:

"Be ye ashamed O ye husbandmen; howl O ye vine dressers. for the wheat and the barley; for the harvest of the field is perished; the vine is dried up and the fig tree languisheth, the pomegranate tree, even all the trees of the field are withered, because joy is withered away from the sons of men. Gird yourselves ye *priests* and *lament*, and howl ye ministers of the altar; come, lie *all night* in sack cloth ye ministers of my God, for the meat offering and the *drink* offering is withholden from the house of your God."

In this portrait the exact features are seen—in the hypocritical pretensions of Iowa, Kansas and Maine. Instead of giving the people the "Gospel that God preached to Abraham," the cowardly mercenary pulpit exponents, so far as prohibition sentiments control it, wish state and national legislation to effect what the Great God commands them to demand, by authority of his unrepealable statutes.

In the 3 ch, 3 v, .these wonderful words occur: "And they have cast lots for my people and given a boy for a harlot and sold a *girl* for *wine* that they might drink." See 18 v. 2 ch, 19 v: "Yea the Lord will answer and say unto his people, I will send you corn and *wine*, &c. 24 v: "And the floors shall be full of wheat and the fats shall overflow with wine and oil."

AMOS.

Is the next to Joel, 787 years before Christ. His pedigree is superb.

2 ch, 8 v: "They drink the wine of the condemned in the house of their God." 12 v: "But ye give the Nazarites wine to drink, and commanded the prophets saying prophecy not." Read the 6 ch., entire.

The 9 ch, 14 v, has these words: "And I will bring again the captivity of my people Isreal and they shall build the waste cities and inhabit them, and they shall plant vineyards and drink the *wine* thereof."

MICAH.

His prophecy was brief, 730 years before Christ:

"If a man walking in the spirit and falsehood do lie, saying, I will prophesy unto thee of wine and of strong drink 'he shall never be the prophet of this people." 6 ch, 15 v: "Thou shalt not drink wine." Wine then was in use but disallowed to a prophet.

HABAKKUK.

2 ch, 5 v: "Yea also he transgresseth by wine," 626 years before Christ.

ZEPHANIAH

Is next, 626 years before Christ. 1 ch, 13 v: "Therefore &c., they shall plant vineyards but not drink the wine thereof."

HAGAI.

See 1 ch, 11 v. Where a number of items &c are forbidden, wine one of them. The same is true of the 2 ch, 12 v.

ZECHARIAH.

See 9 ch, 15 v. also 17 v, which says: "Corn shall make the young man cheerful and new wine the maidens." 10 ch, 7 v: "And they of Ephraim shall be like a mighty man and their hearts shall rejoice as through wine."

MALACHI.

397 years before Christ has these words in 3 ch, 11 v: "And I will rebuke the devourier for your sakes and he shall not destroy the fruit of your grounds nor your vines cast their fruit before the time."

NEW TESTAMENT.

It is an anomalous fact how little importance attaches to the *inspired* teachings of the Old Testament scriptures, with many denominations professing to teach christianity. Some go so far as to set aside the "Old Book" entirely, as of no importance to a correct understanding as to what is necessary to *believe* and *to do* in order to be a christian. Yet the New Testament never changed the condition of a sinner's salvation from the garden of the parentage of the human race; to Patmos, where John saw the hundred and forty-four thousand and the general assembly and church of the first born and an innumerable company of Angels. Directly to the eye of every one concerned on the subject of salvation the *New Testament*, John 5 ch, 39 v, says: "Search the scriptures, for in them ye think ye have eternal life and they are they that testify of ME!! Acts, 17 ch, 11 v, says: "These received the word, with all readiness of mind and searched the *scriptures* daily

PROHIBITION A FALLACY. 91

whether these things were so." St. Paul preached that God foreseeing, he would justify the heathen (all the human race to the end of the world not lineally descended from Jacob)—"preached the gospel before to Abraham." Here we have it that God, Christianity, the Gospel of God and the Gospel of Jesus Christ have ever been the same. And God's method of governing the world admits of no improvement; that he would justify the heathen (Gentiles) through faith, *preached* the gospel before to Abraham. saying, &c. What did he say to Abraham? Well, he said he is the father of every one that believes in Christ as the Savior, unto justification, the forgiveness of his sins. Then, what does the New Testament teach on the subject of Intoxicants. Exactly what has been taught from Lot and Noah to the days of John the Baptist; thence to the closing scene upon Patmos. The use of intoxicants has never been *prevented* by divine enactment. But *Temperance* demanded and *drunkenness* forbidden. But it is a fact that the Old and New Testament scriptures, thunder denunciations against offences and offenders, against the laws of morality and christianity, a thousand fold more dishonoring to God, and the best interest of mankind than drunkenness of any degree and limit of continuance.

The great apostle Paul, Acts, 24 ch, 25 v, "reasoned before Felix, of righteousness, *Temperance* and a judgment to come." But it is not to be found, that he ever, nearly or remotely, clearly or obscurely reasoned in favor of a prohibitory local option or total abstinence civil statutes to *prevent* the *existence* of intoxicants. He *reasoned* to the Ephesians, 5 ch, 18 v. Be not *drunk* with *wine* wherein is excess, that is, an excessive use of *wine* produces drunkenness which the apostle forbids. That he did not mean prohibition or total abstinence is clear, from his advice to his son, Timothy, 5 ch, 23 v, which reads: "Drink no longer *water* but use a little *wine* for thy stomach's sake and thine often infirmities." See 3 ch, 8 v, which says: "Likewise must the deacons be grave not double tongued, not given to MUCH *wine*, not greedy of filthy lucre." Hear this authority once more, 1st Timothy, 3 ch, 2 v: "A bishop then must be blameless, the husband of one wife, vigilant, *sober*, of good behavior, given to hospitality, apt to teach, not *given* to *wine*, no striker, not greedy of filthy lucre, patient, not a brawler; not covetous." See 1st Thessalonians, 5 ch, 7 v: "They that be drunken are drunken in the night, but let us who are of the day be SOBER." Here is gospel temperance, but no nonsensical prohibition foolishness. Once more this blazing star of inspiration speaks, says to *Titus*, 1 ch, 7 v: "For a Bishop must be blameless, as the steward of God. Not self-willed, not soon angry, not *given* to *wine*, not given to filthy lucre; but a lover of hospitality, a lover of good men, *sober*, just, holy, *Temperate*." We next direct attention to the wholesouled

APOSTLE PETER.

Hear him, 4 ch, 3 v: "For the time past of our life, may suffice us to have wrought the will of the Gentiles when we walked in lasciviousness, lusts, *excess* of WINE, reveling, banqueting and *abominable idolatries*." To the eye of a prohibitionist, whether male or female, "*Gospel* temperance" lecturers, nothing in this catalogue of immoralities has ever been observed except the "excess of wine." At any rate they never mention them in their temperance harangues. Observe that the offence was not the *use* of wine but its *excessive* use. Does a prohibitionist know the difference between the rational use of food and eating to gluttony? It might be in order for the *immense* Talmage, of Brooklyn Tabernacle notority, to furnish as a benefit of moral ideas to his world wide hearers, a sermon on what the Apostle Peter meant by the terms in this text, "lasciviousness, lusts, reveling, banqueting and abominable IDOLATRIES." *His* sentiments (and they have been but only *his* sentiments) as the teachings of christianity are that "whoever uses swine meat regularly becomes *polluted* in soul and diseased in body," and gives as proof of the truth of this assumption that ever since the devils that possessed two of the Gergesenes were driven out of them by Christ and went into a herd of many swine that ran violently down a steep place into the sea and perished." Mat. 8 ch, 22 v: "the devil has been in the swine" (hogs). The chances are that Dr. Talmage in this conclusion is about as near the truth of gospel teachings, as he has been on the subject of "gospel prohibition temperance." We will mention another instance of the incoherency and rhapsodical nonsense of this distinguished sentimentalist in substituting his sentimental vagaries for gospel truth; and doubtless presumes that whatever he says or writes will find acceptance and approval as gospel truth and semi-divine. This distinguished pulpiteer has recently been to *Athens* and says he preached on Mars Hill. Alludes to the fact of St. Paul preaching on Mars Hill. I have read Dr. Talmage's sermon and thought singular that his text was not any of the utterances of St. Paul on that occasion. His sermon was the tamest I had ever read from his imaginative pen. We have often read St. Paul's sermon on Mars Hill which, under the circumstances of its delivery is the grandest. the most heroic, manly, historical, logical and theological that can be found in any language of the world. If Dr. Talmage mentioned the type of his audience we do not have it in mind at this time. But the type of St. Paul's auditors was the most extraordinary ever addressed by any minister of the Gospel of Jesus Christ. Athens was a seminary of philosophers whose object was to oppose belief in religion. Paul was not there as a criminal. but was invited by the Areophagite—the Supreme Court of twelve Judges—men of the most distinguished families in Athens. At this audience were gathered senators, philosophers, rhetoricians, statesmen, &c., &c. Paul was a man without fustian or foolishness in his talk, and in one short sermon triumphantly established the truth of Christianity at the most learned, talented, wealthy and idolatrous communities then existing. With reference to this occasion Dr. Talmage in his late visit to Athens, says: "Paul turned his eye toward Corinth after he left the mobocracy of Athens." No mob occurred during Paul's preaching, or stay at Athens. There is no account of such an event in the Acts of the Apostles. Dr. Talmage further says in his late book from "MANGER TO THRONE," page 22.. "No wonder that meeting broke up in a riot, and that Paul had to *clear out*, and go to Corinth, from which *we* came day before yesterday. It was not yesterday afternoon, so much that the wind fluttered the leaves of my Bible, as I was speaking about that *address* of Paul on Mars Hill, as it was *emotion* that shook the book when that apostolic theme rose before my imagination. I obtained a block of stone from Mars Hill to be sent to Brooklyn for the pulpit-table, in our new church, now building. But has *this Paul* nothing to do with the blest One, whose life I am trying to write? Yes, Paul was Jesus Christ's man. Mars Hill shall be to us only a stepping stone to Golgotha." Our comment on the above is this, that there is not in the realm of ideas, nor labyrinth of words, the equal of the nonsensicle twaddle, incoherency of parts, and tumblement and jumblement of subjects as are contained in the paragraph quoted: In self-sufficiency, self-importance, and self-glorification, it transcends the vanity-bloated, self-appointed comforters that visited the illustrious man of Us, "whose name was *Job*;" whose sympathetic *emotions* were fully relieved in telling the distressed patriarch that *they only* were left to tell him, that every sheep that he had sheared, and every camel that bore a burden, every ox that pulled with a yoke, and every species of his stock, had been either killed or stolen; and finally one of his comforters came, and said he only had escaped a terrible cyclone that had blown down their houses and killed all his children. See Job, 1st ch. And but for Dr. Talmage, the commonwealth of Israel and all Christendom, could have ever known that St. Paul's preaching at Athens, "broke up in a riot," and that "Paul had to *clear out* and go to Corinth" for the safety of his life, we presume.

We challenge the pulpit of the world to find anything in that Apostle's preaching to support such a monstrous reminiscense. Paul's preaching at Mars Hill, resulted, from one sermon, in a genuine revival of gospel christianity; insomuch he was invited to return. Among his converts was Dyonisius the Areophagite—one of the twelve Judges of Athens Supreme Court; and Damaris, a woman of great distinction; but not reported as the president of the Woman's Christian Prohibition Temperance Union; and many others, but none of them prohibitionists.

However nearly alike as expounders of Gospel Truth, Dr. Talmage and St. Paul may be, there is this distinct difference, Dr. Talmage is a prohibitionists, St. Paul was not. Possibly, some may think Dr. Talmage understands the science and philosophy of christianity better than the hero of Athens—St. Paul—did. "To your own master you stand or fall." Another distinct difference is manifest:—St. Paul advertised the greatness of God, and Jesus Christ as the Saviour of the world. Dr. Talmage advertises the greatness of the Brooklyn Tabernacle, of which he is the supreme head.

As to Dr. Talmage "trying to write the life of the Blest One." We suggest such a "life" would be a work of supererogation. The life of Christ has already been written with a perspicuity and by authority that admits of no duplication, diminution or addition. One *New Testament* is enough!!! The ambition and vanity to prompt such a purpose would have a larger remuneration, financially, to its author and publisher than any moral and spiritual benefit to be derived by the reader to whom it would be dedicated. After all, it may have been the wind that rustled the leaves of the Bible and not his emotional agitation. In this, however, the Dr. shall have the benefit of the doubt.

What is meant by "Mars Hill shall be our stepping stone to Golgotha," remains to be explained in Dr. Talmage's "Life of the Blest One."

We next invite attention to the existence and use of intoxicants during the life of the Lord Jesus Christ. In Mathew 26 ch, 26-29 v, inclusive is the proof of what we affirm: "And as they were eating, Jesus took bread and blessed it and broke it and gave it to the disciples, and said, take, eat, this is my body. And he took the cup and gave thanks, and gave it to them, saying Drink, ye, all of it; for this is my blood of the New Testament which is shed for many for the remission of sins. But I say unto you I will not *drink* henceforth of this *fruit of the wine* until that day when I *drink* it *new* with you in my father's kingdom." It was at the supper table that the wine was used as well as the bread, and thanks were offered to the Great God for the use of the wine by Christ himself, and then to say that Jesus Christ was a total abstainer, a local optionist or prohibitionist, renders it beyond comprehension why he should have adopted wine for the purpose of sacramental remembrance of his atoneing death.

Next we notice Luke, 5 ch, 37, 38 and 39 v, said Christ: "No man putteth new wine into old bottles, else the new wine will burst the bottles and be spilled, and the bottles shall perish. But new wine must be put into new bottles and both are preserved. No man also having drunk *old wine* straight way desireth new, for he saith the *old is better.*" But why is it better? For no other reason than one is fit to drink with a relishable appreciation from the stimulation. It produces action to the mind and muscle, and the other is not, any more than a green grape is not relishable to the appetite which the ripe grape supplies. But Christ makes the distinction in favor of the use of the *old wine.*

Look at the following, Luke 7 ch, 33-34 v: "For John the Baptist came neither eating bread nor *drinking wine*; and ye say he hath a devil. The son of man is come, eating and *drinking*, and ye say, behold a gluttonous man and a *wine* bibber." Was there any total abstinence, local option or prohibition in the solid and unsullied character of Jesus

Christ? Neither!! Never. As all the readers of this book are to a greater or less extent readers of the New Testament, we need only to refer to a number of passages, where the subject of wine is treated without quoting the text in full. See Mathew 9 ch, 17 v. Here you have Christ's argument about new wine and old bottles. See 11 ch, 10-19 v. In 21 ch, 33 v, &c, is given the history of a householder and his vineyard and his *wine* press, &c, See 24 ch, 38-49 v.

MARK.

See 2 ch, 22 v. 12 ch, 1 v. 14 ch, 23-25 v. 15 ch, 23 v.

LUKE.

1 ch, 15 v, says "He shall be great in the sight of the Lord and shall drink neither wine nor strong drink." Then wine and strong drink did exist at the birth and during the life of the Lord Jesus. 5 ch,

30-39 v, is a slam against presumptious prohibition. See 7 ch, 33 v. In 10 ch, 33- 34 v, Christ gives the account of the good Samaritan, whose conduct He approved because he had bound up his wounds, "in oil and *wine.*" 12 ch, 45 v, 22 ch, 18-30 v, 18 v says: "I will not drink of the fruit of the wine until the kingdom of God shall come." Read it all.

JOHN,

The 4th Evangelist forever settles the question as to Christ's sentiments on the use of wine. 2 ch, 1-9 v, gives the marriage in Cana of Galilee. His mother and his disciples were present. The governor of the feast was present and a great many besides. *Wine* was a cardinal element in this festivity, and become exhausted. Christ produced a new and an abundant supply of better wine than had been used on that occasion. The reader that will turn to the 2 ch. of John and read it, will never again question the fact that *intoxicating* wine was produced at that wedding, but no report of anyone "tarrying too long" at the inebriating bowl. Allusion to this occasion is found 4 ch, 46 v: "So Jesus came again into Cana of

Galilee where *He made* the *water* WINE." Allusion to Peter on the day of penticost in Acts has already been made. Where he defended his rapturous converts against the charge of being drunk. From this event it cannót be disputed that the means to produce intoxication did actually exist. Hence there was then no law of prohibition?

SUPPLEMENTARY.

By accident the following text was lost from its proper place in the recitations from the book of

PROVERBS.

23 ch, 29-32 v: "Who hath woe? Who hath sorrow? Who hath contentions? Who hath babbling? Who hath wounds without cause? Who hath redness of eyes?" The answer, 30 v, says: "They that

tarry long at the *wine*, they that go to seek mixed wine. 31 v: Look not upon the wine when it is red, when it giveth its color in the cup, when it moveth itself aright. 32 v: At last it biteth like a serpent, and stingeth like an adder." While no prohibition lecturer has failed to quote the above to support prohibition, there is no prohibition in it, none whatever. It is strictly a temperanc lecture of Solomon to his subjects. *Tarrying long* at the wine and seeking mixed wine and looking upon or using the wine when it is red, &c, which is forbidden, is where the woe, and the sorrow, the babbling, redness of eyes and contentions come from, and not from the rational use of wine. At all events this was no statutory prohibition. Moreover how many thousands of gorgeously furnished parlors with glittering chandeliers have witnessed debauches, and disaster to character and happiness for life, a result of the parties *"tarrying"* long after they should have been in the quiet embraces of morpheus in their apartments at their respected homesteads. While prohibitionists are seeking to destroy the existence of saloons they should have an eye to abate some of the abuses of parlors.

www.ingramcontent.com/pod-product-compliance
Lightning Source LLC
Chambersburg PA
CBHW031406160426
43196CB00007B/919